In the same series by PatrickGeorge:

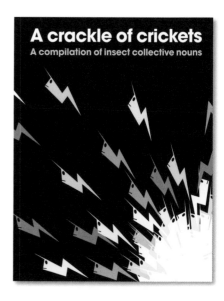

© PatrickGeorge 2012
Second edition revised
First published in the United Kingdom in 2009

Illustrated, designed and published by
PatrickGeorge
46 Vale Square
Ramsgate
Kent CT11 9DA
United Kingdom

www.patrickgeorge.biz

ISBN 978-1-908473-02-8

British Library Cataloguing in Publication Data.
A catalogue record for this book is available from the British Library.

Printed in China.

A filth of starlings

A compilation of bird collective nouns

PatrickGeorge

A parliament of owls

Calling and answering each other across the forest floor, the wise owls debate the issues of the night. Preferring to hunt from dusk till dawn, they often take on prey far heavier than themselves. Able to use their astute hearing and all-round vision, they are always watching their backs.

A paddling of ducks

Gliding or darting through the water, every movement the duck makes seems effortless and yet under the water their feet are paddling away. Heading upstream can be harder work but their webbed feet are just made for the job!

A confusion of guinea fowl
The guinea fowl is commonly known as night watchman amongst other poultry. Fearing strangers and preferring familiarity, it will shriek harshly and loudly if disturbed by an intruder in the night, causing widespread confusion.

A murder of crows

It has a murderous look in the eye and caws into the mist… Fearless yet wary – commonly found in graveyards and old ruins, this is one of the cleverest and most adaptable of birds. Often seen trespassing, it quickly gains confidence and seizes what it can.

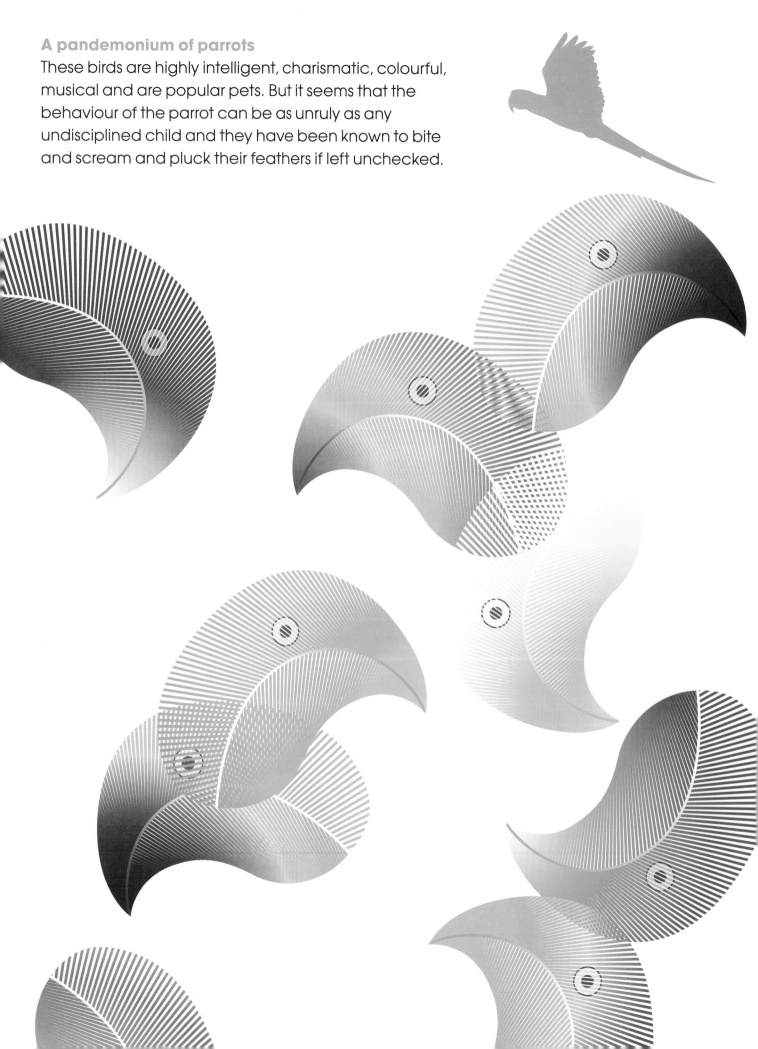

A pandemonium of parrots

These birds are highly intelligent, charismatic, colourful, musical and are popular pets. But it seems that the behaviour of the parrot can be as unruly as any undisciplined child and they have been known to bite and scream and pluck their feathers if left unchecked.

A huddle of penguins

Most penguins like to keep their distance, but if you
are an Emperor penguin enduring the coldest winters,
you choose to huddle together to keep warm. Keeping
cosy also means keeping their feet warm, so they rock
backwards on their heels, supporting themselves with their
tail feathers, which have no blood flow and so lose no heat.

A clutch of chicks

Cute, fluffy and irresistible to many, when you see a chick you probably feel the urge to reach out and clutch it to your chest. The term 'clutch' also refers to a single amount of eggs laid by one bird in its nest.

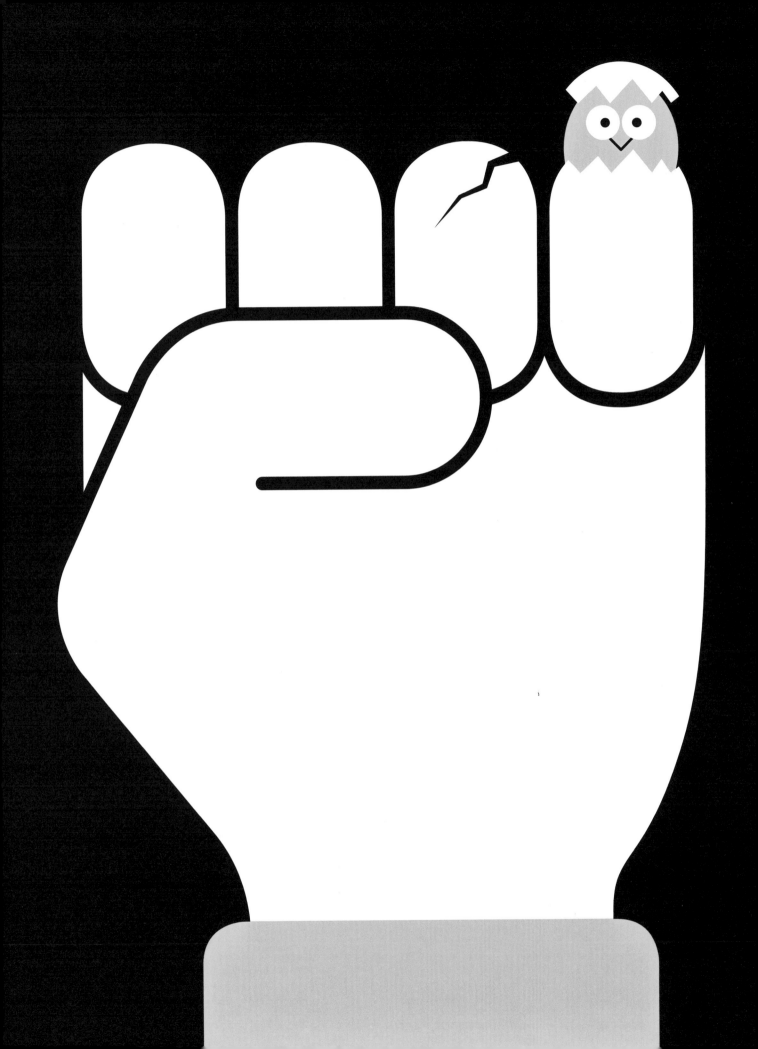

A kit of pigeons

As soldiers packed their kit bags and went to war, so did
the pigeons. In World War One, dogs and pigeons were used
as messengers. In the Second World War, they were used
extensively for sending messages and carrying equipment
and, as a result, helped to save thousands of lives.

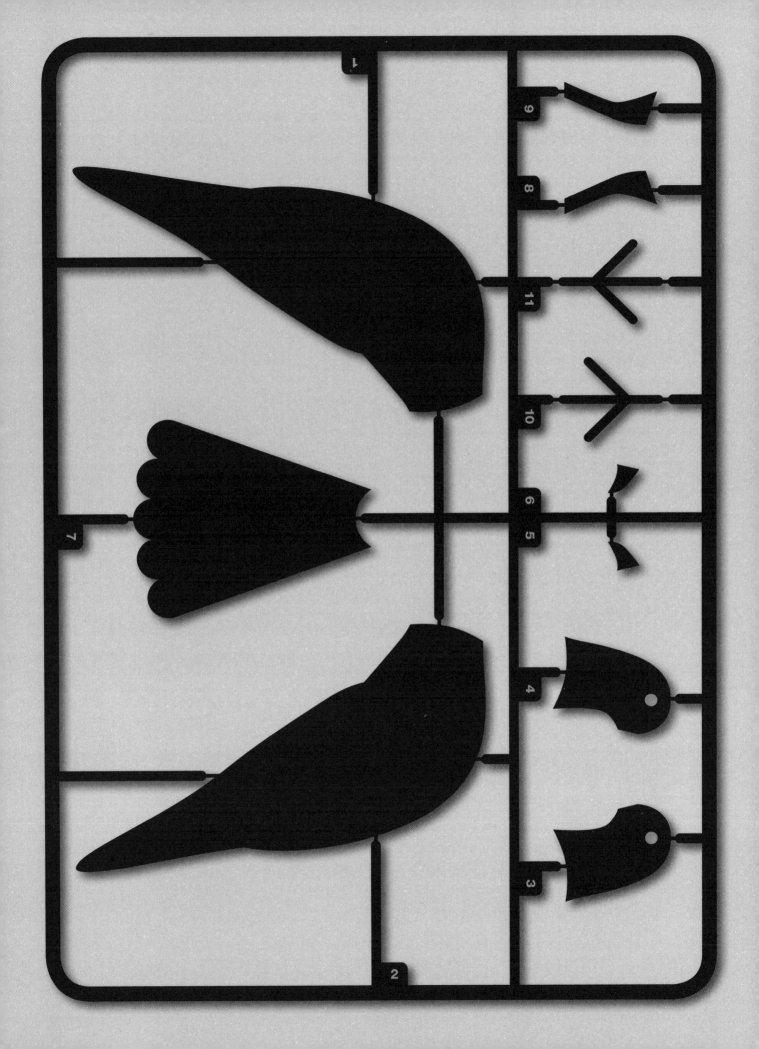

A party of jays

Known as 'garrulus glandarius', the garrulous, loud, strikingly colourful Eurasian jay could be perceived as a party animal whereas in fact it is a shy bird. Known for its love of acorns, it can be seen hiding them far and wide in preparation for the winter.

A chatter of budgerigars

The budgerigar can chatter and whistle tunes all day long. Often having its own favourite music, it loves to listen and learn. From Australia, this bird – one of the most popular birds to be kept in captivity – is by nature extremely nomadic and likes wide, open spaces.

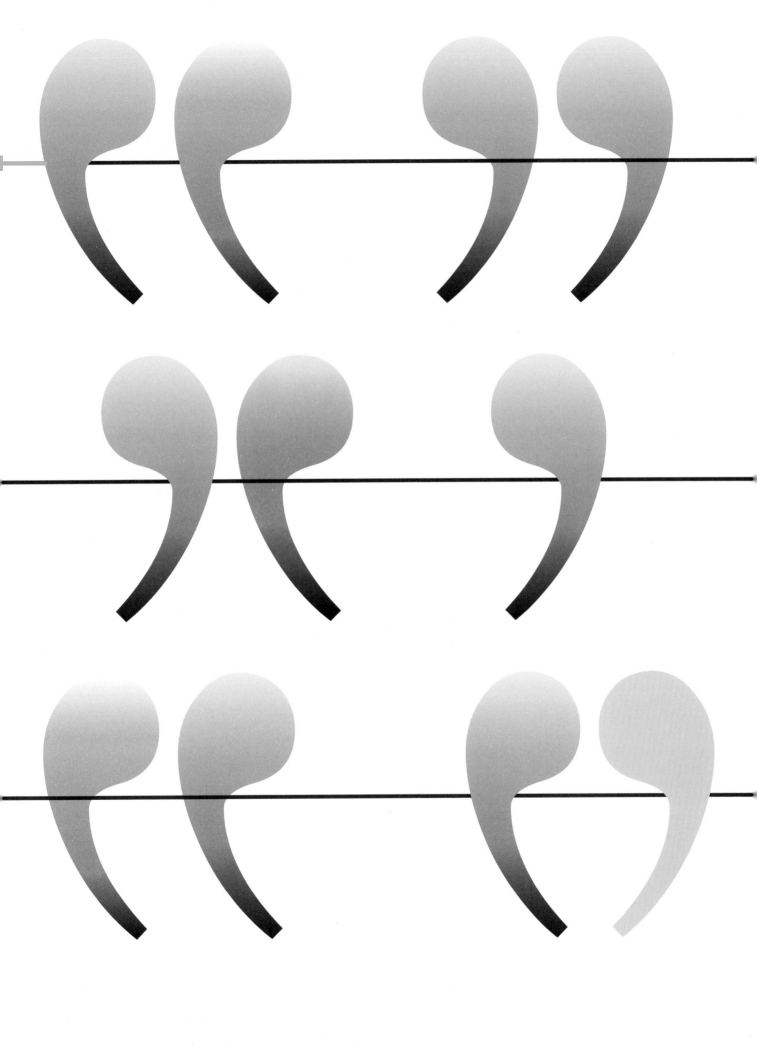

A descent of woodpeckers

Not surprisingly, the woodpecker is designed for maximum grip and stability when up a tree. With its four toes (two facing forwards and two backwards), its sharp nails, and tripod-like tail feathers, it descends upon a tree with utmost confidence. But despite its tenacity, many woodpecker species are critically endangered – a sad descent indeed.

A lamentation of swans

Contrary to former belief, the beautiful white mute swan is not mute. References in classical literature mention the silent swan that would sing beautifully before it died, hence the phrase 'swan song'.

A kettle of hawks

Swirling and spiralling, hawks seek out the rising air thermal during migration. Hungry for its prey, the white-tailed hawk plucks insects from the rising smoke of the wildfire. And a pair indulge in aerial acrobatics, steamily circling, diving and soaring during courtship.

A flamboyance of flamingoes
Gorgeously coloured, ostentatious and showy:
a flamboyant bird turned pink by the blue-green
algae that it eats. It spends its day feeding, preening,
resting and bathing and likes to posture and show
off its vibrant feathers in ritualised breeding displays.

A filth of starlings

These common birds, *sturnus vulgaris*, live in flocks and
are noisy, gregarious and messy. In winter they gather daily
to roost in the treetops, creating unwelcome filth below.
Yet if you look up into the sky each day at dusk in winter,
you will see them – a swirling black cloud, swooping and
regrouping – one of nature's constants amongst the chaos.

A circus of puffins

With its teardrop red and black eye-markings and brightly coloured bill, the puffin is often described as resembling a clown. Most of the year their bills are dull and are only colourful during the breeding season when they grow an extra decorative layer.

A storytelling of ravens

With its capacity for mimicry and its expressive call, the raven would make a good storyteller. A bird of legend and poetry, it is widely associated with evil and doom. But the raven is intelligent and playful and larger than life – widely seen in urban and natural settings, hunting and scavenging wherever it can.

A bouquet of pheasants

If a male pheasant were human, it would be sure to offer its female some beautiful flowers, such is its loyalty during the breeding season. The male will fiercely guard its harem of hens, fighting other males off to keep them away. And its vibrantly coloured feathers make a fine bouquet!

A chime of wrens

A dog barks, a lawn mower hums, a car goes racing by
and over it all the loud trill of the wren can be heard.
For such a tiny bird, it has an incredibly loud voice and
complex song which, like the chime of the church bell,
is a sound we associate with the British countryside.

A flock of geese

Birds of a feather flock together. Geese remain in flocks year-round, except while nesting. Couples tend to mate for life and jointly they protect their young in the nest. Even in migration they maintain contact, forming impressive, aerodynamic V-formations, noisily honking and stopping at designated rest stops along the way!